D1410942

WORLD WAR I
12 THINGS TO KNOW

www.12StoryLibrary.com

12-Story Library is an imprint of Peterson Publishing Company and Press Room Editions.

Produced for 12-Story Library by Red Line Editorial

Photographs ©: Bettmann/Corbis, cover, 1; Red Line Editorial, 4; Bain News Service/Library of Congress, 5, 7, 8, 9, 16, 22, 24; Photo12/UIG/Getty Images, 6; Library of Congress, 10, 15, 18; AS400 DB/Corbis, 11; Keystone View Company/Library of Congress, 12, 28; Berliner Verlag/Archiv/picture-alliance/dpa/AP Images, 14; AP Images, 17, 20, 23, 27, 29; US Army Air Force/AP Images, 19; William de Leftwich Dodge/Library of Congress, 25; W. L. King/Library of Congress, 26

Content Consultant: Justin Quinn Olmstead, Ph.D., Assistant Professor of History, Department of History and Geography, University of Central Oklahoma

Library of Congress Cataloging-in-Publication Data
Names: Hinman, Bonnie, author.
Title: World War I : 12 things to know / by Bonnie Hinman.
Other titles: World War I, twelve things to know
Description: Mankato, MN : 12-Story Library, [2017] | Series: America at war | Includes bibliographical references and index. | Audience: Grades 4-6.
Identifiers: LCCN 2016002433 (print) | LCCN 2016002590 (ebook) | ISBN 9781632352705 (library bound : alk. paper) | ISBN 9781632353207 (pbk. : alk. paper) | ISBN 9781621434399 (hosted ebook)
Subjects: LCSH: World War, 1914-1918--Juvenile literature.
Classification: LCC D522.7 .H55 2016 (print) | LCC D522.7 (ebook) | DDC 940.3--dc23
LC record available at http://lccn.loc.gov/2016002433

Printed in the United States of America
Mankato, MN
May, 2016

Access free, up-to-date content on this topic plus a full digital version of this book. Scan the QR code on page 31 or use your school's login at 12StoryLibrary.com.

Table of Contents

War to End All Wars Begins

Before World War I, many European countries had agreements with other countries. The countries would support each other in times of war. There was peace in Europe in early 1914, but it did not last.

On June 28, 1914, Archduke Franz Ferdinand and his wife, Sophie, were shot and killed in Sarajevo. This city was the capital of the province of Bosnia-Herzegovina. Austria-Hungary annexed Bosnia-Herzegovina in 1908. The archduke was the heir to the throne of Austria-Hungary.

Serbia shared a border with Bosnia-Herzegovina. Many Serbs lived in the newly annexed province.

This map shows European alliances during World War I.

Central Powers
Allied Powers
Neutral

Norway
Sweden
Denmark
Great Britain
Netherlands
Germany
Russia
Belgium
Luxembourg
Austria-Hungary
France
Switzerland
Italy (joined 1915)
Romania (joined 1915)
Serbia
Montenegro
Bulgaria (joined 1915)
Spain
Albania
Greece (joined 1917)
Ottoman Empire
Portugal
Algeria
Tunisia

25

Number of Bosnian citizens tried for planning the assassination of the archduke.

- Before World War I, many European countries had support agreements with each other.
- Gavrilo Princip, a Bosnian Serb, killed Archduke Franz Ferdinand on June 28, 1914.
- Austria-Hungary declared war against Serbia on July 28, 1914.
- The United States said it would remain neutral.

A Bosnian Serb named Gavrilo Princip killed the archduke. Princip was part of a group called the Black Hand. The group hoped to create a union between Serbia and Bosnia-Herzegovina.

Austria-Hungary demanded Serbia punish members of the Black Hand. But Serbia did not agree. So Austria-Hungary declared war on Serbia on July 28, 1914. Russia sent troops to support Serbia. Germany saw this as a threat since it had an alliance with Austria-Hungary.

So Germany responded to the threat by sending in troops as well. France had an agreement with Russia and was soon at war with Germany as a result. Great Britain declared war on Germany in support of France. Soon, most European countries found themselves at war in support of their alliances.

World War I began as support for the two sides grew. Germany, Austria-Hungary, and their allies made up the Central Powers. Great Britain, France, Belgium, and Russia made up the Allied Powers.

President Woodrow Wilson said the United States would remain neutral. Many people thought the war would be over by Christmas. That did not happen.

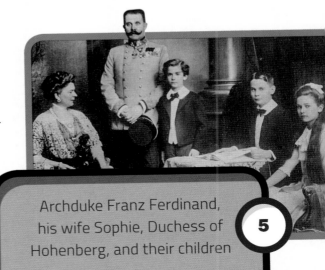

Archduke Franz Ferdinand, his wife Sophie, Duchess of Hohenberg, and their children

5

United States Declares War on Germany

The war dragged on and on. British and French soldiers fought German soldiers at the First Battle of the Marne, the Battle of Verdun, and many others. These battles took place on the Western Front, in France and Belgium. Russia attacked Germany and Austria-Hungary on the Eastern Front.

US citizens still did not want to go to war. But many changed their minds in January 1917. Germany sent a coded message to its ambassador in Mexico. The message was called the Zimmermann Telegram, after the German foreign minister who sent it. The British intercepted the telegram. They decoded it and released the message. It proposed that Mexico attack the United States after joining the war as a German ally. Americans were outraged. President Wilson

Soldiers at Verdun, France, in 1916

admitted war now seemed unavoidable.

On January 31, 1917, Germany announced its submarines would sink any ships entering the war zone around Great Britain. This included US vessels. The announcement made it clear that being neutral was no longer possible. Attacking neutral vessels was an act of war. The United States declared war on Germany on April 6, 1917.

Arthur Zimmermann was the German foreign secretary from 1916 to 1917.

29

Number of submarines in the German U-boat fleet at the beginning of the war.

- Germany sent a message to Mexico asking it to attack the United States.
- On January 31, 1917, Germany declared it would sink all ships in the war zone around Great Britain, including those from neutral nations.
- The United States declared war on Germany on April 6, 1917.

NAMING THE WAR

During the war, Americans did not call the conflict in Europe World War I. They called it the European War, World War, or Great War. President Woodrow Wilson called it the War to End All Wars. In 1941, the United States entered a new war in Europe. President Franklin D. Roosevelt publicly called that conflict World War II. After that, the war of 1914 to 1918 was called World War I, or the First World War.

United States Scrambles to Prepare for War

The United States was not ready to go to war. In April 1917, the total number of men in both the regular army and the National Guard was approximately 200,000. Military leaders estimated it would take a million soldiers to win the war. They wondered where they would find 800,000 more men to join the army.

President Wilson and his advisers decided a draft was necessary.

There was no other way to enlist so many soldiers in such a short amount of time. On May 18, 1917, Congress passed the Selective Service Act. All men between the ages of 21 and 31 were required to register. From this pool of names, men were chosen randomly to enlist in the army.

Wilson chose Major General John J. "Black Jack" Pershing

Between 1917 and 1918, approximately 24 million US men registered for the draft.

General Pershing (saluting) arrived in France to an enthusiastic welcome.

as commander of the American Expeditionary Forces (AEF) in Europe. Pershing left for Great Britain via ship on May 28, 1917. From there, he traveled to France.

Pershing got a warm welcome. The Allied Powers were tired and discouraged. They hoped the coming of the "Yanks," as Americans were often called, would end the war.

The first US troops arrived in France on June 26, 1917. Many of the soldiers were untrained and not highly disciplined. When they marched in a July 4 parade in Paris, local citizens did not seem to care about these things. They crowded the streets to cheer, "*Vive les Américains! Vive Pershing! Vive les États Unis.*" It meant, "Long live the Americans! Long live Pershing! Long live the United States!" It was an outstanding start for the Americans. The hard part came later.

14,000
Number of US troops who landed in France on June 26, 1917.

- The United States had 200,000 soldiers available in 1917.
- The Selective Service Act passed on May 18, 1917, requiring men ages 21 to 31 to register for the draft.
- The first US troops landed in France on June 26, 1917.

Yanks Have Long Wait

The AEF soldiers did not head straight for the front lines when they arrived in France. Instead, they went to training camps. They spent many months there. The troops learned how to use a bayonet, how to salute, and how to use open warfare techniques.

General Pershing thought most AEF troops would not be trained well enough to fight before 1919. The British and French military leaders strongly disagreed. They wanted Americans to become part of French and British units on the front right away.

General Pershing refused to break up his forces. He insisted the AEF go into battle as a US unit. He would not allow them to be split up between the French and British.

The flow of US soldiers into combat zones began in the autumn of 1917. Troops began three months of training before going to the front lines. Then, they spent 10 days at a time there as a trial experience. The French 18th Division trained these

General Pershing insisted AEF troops needed full training before serving on the front lines.

THINK ABOUT IT

US soldiers who arrived in France had much to learn in training camps. What were some of the skills they learned? Which skill do you think was most important?

650,000

Number of US soldiers General Pershing expected to have in France by July 1918.

- The AEF soldiers headed to training camps when they arrived in France.
- General Pershing wanted US troops to serve as a unit.
- The French 18th Division trained US troops in trench warfare.
- The first US combat deaths occurred on November 3, 1917.

US troops in trench warfare. US battalions rotated in and out of the frontline trenches for training. The First Division troops who arrived in late June took part in their first trial on the front lines in October.

The first Americans were killed in combat on November 3, 1917, near Bathelémont, France. They had just completed their training and had been sent to a quiet combat zone. The plan was for them to gain experience in the trenches. It was not likely they would face harsh fighting in this region. But the Germans attacked. Three men died, and 11 were taken as prisoners.

Pershing agreed to allow the 369th Infantry Regiment, an African-American unit, to fight with French units.

5

Americans Jump into the Trenches

Trench warfare was used to fight the Great War. Vast networks of trenches formed on either side of the imaginary line that separated the Allies from the Central Powers. The area between enemy trenches was called "no man's land."

On the Western Front, trench systems were 460 miles (740 km) long. They went from the Belgian coast to Switzerland. The Eastern Front had a similar trench system. But it was not as well developed or used.

Trenches were filthy and rat-infested. They were cold or hot, depending on the weather, and a dangerous place to be. War on the Western Front in

US soldiers leave a trench in response to a bugle call to charge.

1917 was stalled. Both sides fought from their trenches, and many men were killed or wounded trying to cross no man's land. But neither side advanced to push the other side back.

General Pershing disagreed with the European system of trench warfare. He trained US troops to attack, as well as defend. Pershing did not think enemies firing back and forth at each other from trenches could win the war. But he knew US troops would sometimes have to fight from the trenches.

Throughout the long, cold winter of 1917 to 1918, AEF troops trained in the trenches. As winter passed, more and more US troops poured into Europe and went to training camps.

STORMTROOPERS

Stormtroopers were elite German soldiers. They were specially trained to break through the weak points in the Allied lines. Stormtroopers moved quickly and with very little gear. They had a variety of weapons beyond the standard rifle most troops were given. One example was the first lightweight machine gun.

200
Number of yards (183 m) separating enemies from each other in "no man's land."

- A line of trenches stretched across Europe from Belgium to Switzerland.
- General Pershing insisted US soldiers train in attack tactics, as well as in trench warfare.
- AEF soldiers trained in the trenches during the winter of 1917 to 1918.
- Germany began a spring offensive on March 21, 1918.

13

6

Germany Pushes toward Paris

In 1917, Russia withdrew from the war. Until then, the German army had been divided between the two fronts. With Russia out of the way, Germany could shift troops from the Eastern Front to the Western Front.

On March 21, 1918, Germany launched poison gas shells into the British front lines northeast of the Somme River in northeastern France. The British forces retreated. This was the first of five German offensives launched in the spring and summer of 1918.

The German offensives were successful at first. The front lines gradually moved toward Paris as British and French forces gave up ground. Allied leaders became desperate for Pershing to bring US troops into the fight.

Pershing stuck to his decision

German and Russian soldiers after Germany and Russia signed a ceasefire agreement in December 1917

GAS ATTACKS

Soldiers used different kinds of chemicals in the war. These included chlorine and phosgene gases, which attacked the lungs. Gas masks offered some protection. But they could not completely protect troops from mustard gas. This gas blistered the skin. It also caused temporary or permanent blindness. And it could cause internal damage to the lungs and other organs.

500,000
Number of German troops moved from the Eastern Front to the Western Front.

- The first of five German spring offensives began on March 21, 1918.
- Poison gas was used by both the Central Powers and the Allied Powers.
- By May 1, 1918, half a million US troops were in France.

that Americans would enter heavy combat zones only when they were fully trained and as a US unit. By the beginning of May 1918, half a million US soldiers were in France. Some of the units had trained in the trenches, but none had fought in a full-on battle.

The German spring offensives continued, and the Allied forces retreated. General Pershing changed his mind about using US troops as support. The Allies had to stop the Germans before they reached Paris. Pershing decided his men would start fighting on the Western Front.

Gas attacks caused panic as soldiers scrambled to pull on their gas masks.

7

America Fights to Block German Advance

Pershing believed his soldiers were still inexperienced. But he agreed to a small operation. US troops needed to show they were able to fight the enemy. On May 28, 1918, the US Army 28th Infantry moved into position to attack and take Cantigny, which was north of Paris.

The attack on Cantigny was successful, but the price was huge. The French heavy artillery was able to stay on the scene during only the first part of the battle. After that, the artillery moved

to support a different battle. This left the US troops open to fierce counterattacks from the Germans. Approximately 200 US officers and men were killed or missing. Another 669 were wounded in the three-day battle.

US soldiers joined French troops to hold the Germans at Château-Thierry. The Battle of Belleau Wood came next. It lasted from June 6 to June 26, 1918. This battle was a bloody fight that sometimes involved hand-to-hand fighting. The Allies won.

Soldiers used flamethrowers in the Battle of Cantigny.

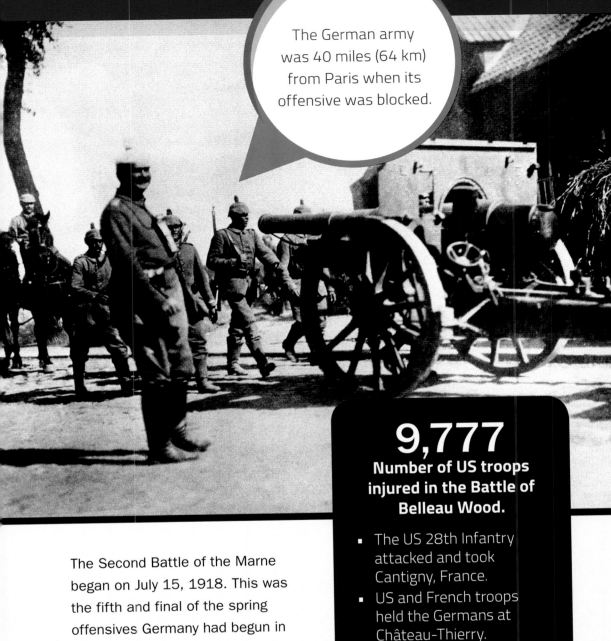

The German army was 40 miles (64 km) from Paris when its offensive was blocked.

9,777
Number of US troops injured in the Battle of Belleau Wood.

- The US 28th Infantry attacked and took Cantigny, France.
- US and French troops held the Germans at Château-Thierry.
- The bloody battle of Belleau Wood lasted from June 6 to June 26, 1918.
- The Second Battle of the Marne began on July 15, 1918, and stopped the German advance.

The Second Battle of the Marne began on July 15, 1918. This was the fifth and final of the spring offensives Germany had begun in March. Along with several French divisions, the American Third Division fought to repel the Germans. By July 20, the Germans began their retreat east. It was the beginning of the end of the war for Germany.

Air War Rages over France and Germany

Both sides used aircraft during the war. At first, they flew over the battlefields and reported enemy moves. They could drop small bombs. But machine guns mounted on the planes did more damage.

The United States did not have its own planes in Europe. US pilots flew French planes. They disrupted enemy supply lines, shot down German observation balloons, and strafed the German trenches. Early in the war, Germans had more and better planes. Over time, Allied pilots got newer planes and more experience.

New fighter planes had just one pilot. They fought fierce battles in the sky called "dogfights." Pilots from both sides fired machine guns at each other while flying through the sky. Some pilots were called flying aces. They were very good at shooting down enemy planes.

Observation balloons powered by hot air or gas would remain in the air for hours at a time.

The most famous German ace was Manfred von Richthofen. He was called "the Red Baron." The Red Baron

25

Age the Red Baron was when he was shot down over British lines.

- Aircraft were first used in the war to report enemy moves.
- Some fighter pilots engaged in dogfights and were called aces.
- The German pilot called the Red Baron shot down 80 Allied planes.
- US ace pilot Eddie Rickenbacker shot down 26 enemy planes.

THINK ABOUT IT

Find a source of information about modern military aircraft. How are they different from those used in World War I?

shot down 80 planes before he was killed on April 21, 1918. He was a hero in Germany. He wrote

his autobiography, *Red Air Fighter*, shortly before he died.

US air ace Captain Eddie Rickenbacker was a former race car driver. He shot down 26 enemy planes, the most of any US pilot. Rickenbacker survived the war and wrote his own memoir, *Fighting the Flying Circus*. It was published in 1919.

Captain Eddie Rickenbacker flew a Spad fighter plane during World War I.

Germans Yield Ground Slowly as They Retreat

At the end of July 1918, General Pershing pushed the other Allied commanders to let him make a major offensive using a separate US army. Finally, they said yes. Pershing then led his newly formed US First Army into battle.

The unit's first test was at St. Mihiel on the southeastern end of the front lines. On September 12, 1918, Pershing's new army attacked. They pushed back the Germans, taking many prisoners on the way. The success at St. Mihiel was a morale booster for all of the Allies. But it was only a dress rehearsal for the next offensive.

The Meuse-Argonne region was a narrow north-south area between the Meuse River on the east and

US Army soldiers in action during the Meuse-Argonne offensive in France

the Argonne Forest on the west. The Germans had heavily fortified the rolling land with machine gun emplacements, artillery positions, and concrete bunkers.

The Meuse-Argonne campaign began on September 26, 1918. The 600,000-man US First Army attacked northward. French, British, and Belgian forces launched similar attacks farther north along the front lines.

General Pershing wanted to drive the Germans back far enough to capture a railway near Sedan, France. It would cut off the main supply network to the German army in France. The fighting was the bloodiest of the entire war.

In spite of many setbacks, the US First Army drove the Germans back foot by foot. Approximately 117,000 US troops were killed or wounded. Supported by French forces, the US troops reached the city of Sedan on November 9, 1918.

450

Number of German guns captured by the Americans at the Battle of St. Mihiel.

- The newly formed US First Army went into battle for the first time on September 12, 1918.
- The Meuse-Argonne campaign began on September 26, 1918.
- US troops reached the city of Sedan on November 9, 1918.

CHER AMI, THE FAMOUS CARRIER PIGEON

With no modern two-way radios, carrier pigeons carried messages between units. The carrier pigeon *Cher Ami,* or Dear Friend, flew out from a US unit on October 4, 1918. The unit was surrounded by the enemy. Cher Ami was carrying a message to the unit's headquarters. The Germans fired on Cher Ami and wounded him. But he delivered the message. He survived, as did the men of the unit he saved.

Germans Surrender

While the armies fought in the Meuse-Argonne battle, rumors began to swirl that armistice talks would take place soon between Allied and German leaders. By November 1918, German soldiers and citizens were sick of war. They wanted to end the fighting.

Germany's leader was Kaiser Wilhelm II. He refused to consider an armistice. The German people protested. Crowds in the streets grew larger and louder. It looked as if there might be a revolution in Germany.

On November 9, 1918, Kaiser Wilhelm II was forced to admit defeat. He abdicated his position and fled to Holland. With the kaiser gone, German leaders declared a republic. Leaders of the new republic agreed to the Allied Powers' terms for an armistice.

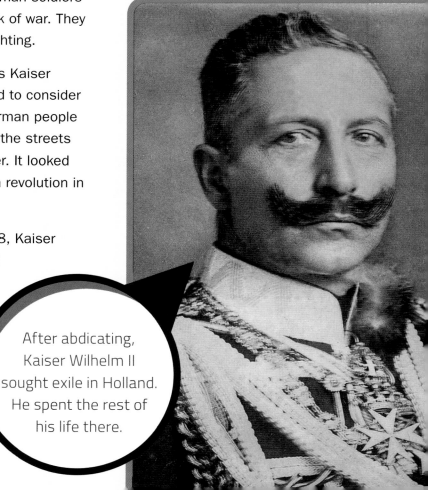

After abdicating, Kaiser Wilhelm II sought exile in Holland. He spent the rest of his life there.

VERSAILLES TREATY TERMS

The terms for peace were harsh. Germany was to withdraw all troops. It had to hand over military equipment. And it had to give up warships and submarines. Allied generals were not sure the new German government would accept the terms. They continued to plan future military operations.

Early on November 11, 1918, representatives from the Allied Powers and Germany signed an armistice agreement. They agreed fighting would officially cease at 11:00 a.m. that day.

Millions of soldiers had died in the war. Countless others were disabled. The war was over, but the results lingered for decades.

10 million

Number of soldiers from all sides estimated to have died in the war.

- At first, German kaiser Wilhelm II refused to consider an armistice.
- He abdicated on November 9, 1918.
- Germany agreed to the terms for an armistice.
- The armistice took effect at 11:00 a.m. on November 11, 1918.

The armistice agreement became effective on the 11th day of the 11th month at 11 a.m. People celebrated around the world.

Paris Peace Conference Brings Hope

On January 18, 1919, the Paris Peace Conference delegates met for the first time in the Palace of Versailles. The three main leaders present were President Wilson, French prime minister George Clemenceau, and British prime minister David Lloyd George. Each leader had different ideas about the terms of the peace treaty they were discussing.

Clemenceau thought Germany should pay for the war, both with money and with the loss of all power. Wilson favored what he called a just peace. He wanted the Germans to be able to decide their own future and form their own government. Lloyd George wanted to find a halfway point between these ideas. But the three leaders all agreed to found a League of Nations.

Peace talks took place in Paris from January to June. After much argument and compromise,

From left to right: British Prime Minister David Lloyd George, Italian Premier Vittorio Orlando, French Premier Georges Clemenceau, and US President Woodrow Wilson at the Paris Peace Conference

On June 28, 1919, Allied leaders met in the Hall of Mirrors at Versailles to watch Germany accept the terms of the Treaty of Versailles.

the Treaty of Versailles was signed on June 28, 1919. Germany did not want to sign the treaty, but it did. It was unhappy with the treaty's harsh terms. It lost a large amount of land, as well as mineral and farm resources. Germany was forced to pay for France to rebuild, and its colonies were given to other countries. As well, Germany's military was drastically reduced.

Wilson came home to the United States to persuade Congress to approve the treaty and join the League of Nations. The treaty suggested member nations would support each other in times of war. But the United States wanted to control its own affairs. It did not want to be drawn into another foreign war. While Congress debated the issue, Wilson suffered a stroke. He was unable to defend the treaty. In the end, Congress refused to ratify it.

32

Number of nations or states that took part in the Paris Peace Conference.

- Paris Peace Conference delegates met for the first time at the Palace of Versailles on January 18, 1919.
- The Treaty of Versailles was signed on June 28, 1919.
- The US Congress refused to approve the treaty.

Tensions Linger

US soldiers streamed home in the months following the armistice. They hoped the battles they fought had been "the war to end all wars."

People in the United States did not want to take part in any more foreign wars. They wanted a drastic reduction in the size of the US armed forces. The number of soldiers had peaked at 4.4 million in late 1918. By 1920, that number had fallen to 344,000.

The people of France and Belgium had much to rebuild. Many of their cities had been destroyed during the war. They did not want to fight in any more wars. The British agreed. Many Allied military leaders thought the Treaty of Versailles could have been harsher to help prevent future wars.

In Germany, citizens were resentful about what they saw as the harsh

Ypres, Belgium, was left in ruins following the war.

100,000

Number of soldiers the German army was limited to by the Treaty of Versailles.

- The number of US soldiers dropped from 4.4 million to 344,000 in two years.
- Germany secretly rebuilt its army and weapons supply.
- Adolf Hitler became Germany's leader in 1933.

THINK ABOUT IT

General Pershing wanted to keep fighting until the German military was crushed. Allied leaders rejected his suggestion. How do you think public opinion in the Allied countries influenced the Allied leaders?

terms of the treaty. The treaty put restrictions on the German military. When Adolf Hitler became the German leader in 1933, he convinced Germans that all of the problems Germany had after the war resulted from the Treaty of Versailles. As a result, Germany abided by few of the terms in the treaty.

The United States and other allies did not take any action when Germany violated the treaty terms. President Franklin D. Roosevelt warned world leaders of

Hitler's defiance. But he was not able to convince them of the danger Hitler presented.

With the Great War still fresh in memory, the Allies appeased Hitler. Tensions were high for another war.

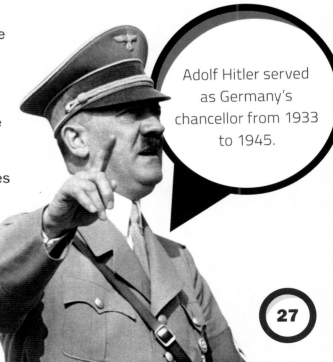

Adolf Hitler served as Germany's chancellor from 1933 to 1945.

12 Key Dates

June 28, 1914
Archduke Franz Ferdinand is gunned down in Sarajevo.

July 28, 1914
Austria-Hungary declares war on Serbia.

April 6, 1917
The United States declares war on Germany.

June 26, 1917
The first US troops arrive in France.

November 3, 1917
The first US troops are killed in combat.

March 21, 1918
Germany launches the first of five spring offensives.

May 28, 1918
Americans attack and take Cantigny, France.

September 12, 1918
The US First Army attacks at St. Mihiel.

September 26, 1918
The Meuse-Argonne campaign begins.

November 11, 1918
The armistice goes into effect at 11 a.m.

December 13, 1918
President Wilson arrives in France for the Paris Peace Conference.

June 28, 1919
The Paris Peace Conference delegates sign the Treaty of Versailles.

Glossary

abdicated
Gave up the throne.

annexed
Added or attached to something larger or more important.

appeased
Gave something to someone to make that person happy or to keep the peace.

armistice
A temporary stopping of a war; a truce between the warring parties.

battalions
Large bodies of troops ready for battle; usually made up of a headquarters and two or more companies or similar units.

bayonet
A narrow, knifelike weapon attached to the end of a gun barrel.

counterattacks
Attacks made in reply to another attack; used to drive back an enemy attack.

Eastern Front
The zone of fighting in countries east of Germany.

neutral
Not taking sides in a dispute or war.

offensive
Attack made to move forward rather than stay and defend a position.

republic
A government in which people elect their representatives.

strafed
Attacked ground troops or positions by airplanes equipped with machine guns.

Western Front
The zone of fighting in countries west of Germany.

For More Information

Books

Adams, Simon. *DK Eyewitness Books: World War I*. New York: DK Children, 2014.

Bausum, Ann. *Stubby the War Dog: The True Story of World War I's Bravest Dog*. New York: National Geographic Children's Books, 2014.

Freedman, Russell. *The War to End All Wars*. New York: Clarion Books, 2010.

Rasmussen, R. Kent. *World War I for Kids: A History with 21 Activities*. Chicago: Chicago Review Press, 2014.

Visit 12StoryLibrary.com

Scan the code or use your school's login at **12StoryLibrary.com** for recent updates about this topic and a full digital version of this book. Enjoy free access to:

- Digital ebook
- Breaking news updates
- Live content feeds
- Videos, interactive maps, and graphics
- Additional web resources

Note to educators: Visit 12StoryLibrary.com/register to sign up for free premium website access. Enjoy live content plus a full digital version of every 12-Story Library book you own for every student at your school.

Index

About the Author

Bonnie Hinman has written more than 35 nonfiction books. She lives in Joplin, Missouri, with her husband, Bill, and near her children and five grandchildren.

READ MORE FROM 12-STORY LIBRARY

Every 12-Story Library book is available in many formats. For more information, visit 12StoryLibrary.com.